N

YES SHE DID!

ENTERTAINMENT

Yes She Did! Entertainment

Copyright © 2014
Published by Scobre Educational
Written by Kirsten Rue

Scobre Educational
2255 Calle Clara
La Jolla, CA 92037

Scobre Operations & Administration
42982 Osgood Road
Fremont, CA 94539

www.scobre.com
info@scobre.com

Scobre Educational publications may be purchased for
educational, business, or sales promotional use.

Cover and layout design by Jana Ramsay
Copyedited by Susan Sylvia
Some photos by Getty Images

ISBN: 978-161570-878-9 (Soft Cover)
ISBN: 978-1-61570-891-8 (Library Bound)

TABLE OF CONTENTS

CHAPTER 1
A MOGUL ON MANY LEVELS

Flipping through the TV channels or looking at magazine covers in the supermarket, Oprah is everywhere. She has her own television station, the OWN network. She publishes *O Magazine.* Even on shows with other stars, such as Ellen Degeneres or Tyra Banks, her influence

"O" GLAMOUR

Oprah stands on stage with the logo of her magazine, TV network, and other businesses.

is there. Most billionaires in the United States are white men who lead or own large corporations. This makes Oprah unique. She is perhaps the most influential woman in entertainment, ever. And she is also the only African-American, female billionaire in the world. Recently, she was named "the richest self-made woman in the world."

Oprah's influence comes not from being a person in an office in a big business, but from being a person who people relate to and like. Of course, she does have an office and a team of employees to help her run her entertainment empire. Oprah's success comes from a very smart—and new—understanding of how to create a brand name for women's entertainment.

On the last day of her talk show, *The Oprah Winfrey Show*, on May 25th, 2011, Oprah kept things simple. While soft guitar music played, she walked through the crowds of her fans, hugging them and squeezing

their hands. "We did it!" she cheered, raising her arms. While many women and men in the audience blinked back tears, Oprah told them her parting was "all sweet. No bitter." Most of all, she encouraged everyone to discover their own dreams in life, and make them a reality. "Everybody has a calling," she said, "and your real job in life is to figure out what that is and get about the business of doing it." Although her own fame came from a television studio, Oprah reminded everyone watching that a person's "studio" is her life. That is the stage where she has to achieve what she wants to

DID YOU KNOW...

Oprah's unique name was actually a product of a misspelling on her birth certificate. It was supposed to be "Orpah," a name from the Bible.

achieve. From the beginning, Oprah's calling has been to inspire others to dream big.

Oprah's path to her calling was not exactly easy. Born in rural Mississippi to a single mother, and later raised in a tough neighborhood in Milwaukee, she often had to face hunger and other hardships. In fact, when she was only 14 years old, she ran away from home. Still, Oprah worked very hard in school, and during her teenage years, her fortunes began to change. "For every one of us that succeeds, it's because there's somebody there to show you the way out. The light doesn't

YEARS OF ACCLAIM

Oprah holding an Emmy award early in her career.

always necessarily have to be in your family; for me it was teachers and school," she says of this time.

By the time she graduated high school, that light had led her to a full college scholarship and a national finish in a drama competition. Oprah's family and friends

Oprah holding an exclusive interview with Lance Armstrong. She often interviews famous and controversial people.

always knew she was destined for the stage…but no one could have guessed how big that stage would become!

Beginning with local radio shows, Oprah made her way into television after executives noticed how well she connected with her audiences. One television critic described her as "hyper, laughable, lovable, [and] soulful." Her big break came in 1986, when the talk show she hosted in Chicago went national. Suddenly, Oprah had the most popular talk show in history! In fact, *The Oprah Winfrey Show* invented the television talk show as we know it today.

When she first began her show, no other women were hosting talk shows. And certainly no other African-American women were hosting them. "How does she do it?" curious people want to know. It seems like Oprah is able to balance multiple careers as she multi-tasks between her different projects. Up before dawn every morning and often in the makeup chair by 7:30, Oprah doesn't know the meaning of "day off." She spends her days in business meetings and sometimes interviewing famous celebrities for her magazine or TV network. She also spends time giving to charity and talking with other leaders. Even when she is tucked into bed, she is still working on picking books to recommend to her readers. At the same time, she tries to make time for friends and healthy living.

Not that Oprah minds the long days. "What I know is, is that if you do work that you love, and the work fulfills you, the rest will come," she says.

CHAPTER 2
BRAVE NEW WORLDS

In Jennifer Lopez's 2002 hit single, "Jenny From The Block," she sang, "Don't be fooled by the rocks that I got, I'm still Jenny from the block." This was Lopez's way of remembering her childhood growing up in a working class neighbor-hood in the Bronx. The daughter of Puerto Rican parents, Lopez and her siblings often acted out song and dance routines in their living room. By age five, Jennifer begged for singing and dancing lessons.

CAMERA-READY
Jennifer Lopez at an event in Puerto Rico.

During her senior year of high school, Lopez auditioned for a small role in a movie and was hooked. Her parents, however, were concerned about her dream, since they didn't think Latina women often had success in show biz. But Lopez was determined. She moved to Manhattan on her own and began auditioning for roles as a back-up dancer. After touring other countries with the popular band New Kids on the Block, Jennifer began dancing on the show *In Living Color*. After two years there, she left the show and found her breakthrough role in the film *Selena*. *Selena* was based on the true story of a very popular Latina singer, and Lopez got the opportunity to practice singing on camera.

After that role, Jennifer's star rose quickly. She began getting cast in higher-profile films, including *Out of Sight*, where she starred with George Clooney. For that film, Jennifer earned

DID YOU KNOW...

Born in Texas, Selena was the top-selling Latin pop star of the 1990s. She helped to pave the way for the success of singers like Jennifer Lopez years later. Tragically, she was murdered by her manager in 1995, cutting her career short.

over $1 million. This was the highest any Latina actress had been paid for a film role. Soon after that, Jennifer Lopez began working on her first album. She knew it would be risky trying to enter the music world from the acting world. Lopez hoped that fans

MEGA-STARS

Jennifer Lopez with George Clooney, her co-star in Out of Sight.

would be able to recognize her singing and dancing talents on her album *On the 6*. The title came from her experience riding the #6 subway train from the Bronx to Manhattan in the early days of her career. Her fears proved to be false, as *On the 6* was a huge hit. Speaking of her album and Puerto Rican heritage, Lopez said: "English is my first language. I grew up here. I was born here, I didn't have a career in Spanish first. I think it [the album] appeals definitely to my generation of people; we grew up in America but had Latin parents or parents of different ethnicity." She has also released hit singles in Spanish, but Lopez wants to appeal to fans who speak any language.

When Lopez released her next album, *J. Lo*, in 2001, it quickly shot up the charts to number one. At the same time, her movie *The Wedding Planner* was released and became the number one movie in America. This made Lopez the first star to have a number one album and movie at the

TWO VOICES

Jennifer Lopez and Marc Anthony sing a duet on-stage in New York.

same time. At this point, one of the biggest movie and music stars in the world, Jennifer Lopez used her fame to create a brand name. She has launched successful fragrances and a clothing line called "The Jennifer Lopez Collection." She has also become a television star as a judge on *American Idol*, and is still touring the world as a performer. Her latest album was another smash hit. Not too bad for Jenny from the block.

Similar to Jennifer Lopez, not many Asian-American women were visible on television when Lisa Ling was growing up in California. The daughter of Chinese and Taiwanese immigrants, Lisa began TV reporting at the very young age of 18. Her parents had divorced when she was only seven years old, which was unusual in her community.

In 2002, she landed a coveted spot co-hosting *The View*, beating out thousands of other women in her audition. After a few years, however, Ling left to pursue international reporting on issues of the environment and injustice. For *National Geographic Explorer* and Oprah's channel, *OWN*, Ling has traveled the world. She is the first woman to host National Geographic's TV program. She has also reported from dangerous locations such as North Korea and inside the Colombian drug wars. Lisa has shone a light on controversial issues such as shark fishing, and violence against women in India and Ghana. Her current title is "Oprah Show Investigative Reporter."

Lisa's younger sister, Laura, is also a journalist. In 2009, Laura Ling and another reporter named Euna Lee were captured and imprisoned while filming on the border of North Korea. After months in captivity, they were released in August of 2009 after Bill Clinton visited the country. The two sisters, thankful to be reunited, collaborated on a book about their experience. *Somewhere Inside: One Sister's Captivity in North Korea and the Other's Fight to Bring Her Home* is the memoir that shares their experiences. While her younger sister fought to survive in captivity, Lisa Ling used her influence in top-secret negotiations. The phone calls between the two journalist sisters became the main way that the U.S. and North Korean governments communicated over releasing the captives.

SMILE FOR THE CAMERA

Lisia Ling smiles for the camera during the 2011 TCA Winter Press Tour.

TENSE SCENE

News teams and families waiting for Laura Ling and Euna Lee to arrive home.

Like a true reporter, Lisa Ling wants to keep covering the story that led to her sister's experience. "I have become even more determined than ever to try and raise awareness. There's a real crisis, and we continue to hope that people, through Laura's and Euna's experience, will want to become more aware of this humanitarian crisis on the border of North Korea and China." Both women remain bravely committed to reporting on justice issues around the world despite this tough time.

CHAPTER 3
THE WRITE STUFF

Historically, women tend to buy and read more fiction than men. In fact, some of the first "best-selling" authors were women who wrote in the 19th century, sometimes using male pen names. Still, female authors often feel that the writing world takes them for granted. A successful author named Jennifer Weiner has pointed out that men's books usually win more awards than women's books. She also noticed that for every women's book that is reviewed in a major

newspaper, men's books usually receive far more space. How can that be changed?

J.K. Rowling, the author of the extremely popular *Harry Potter* series, has helped give more power to women in publishing. Harry Potter, the brave and clever wizard at the center of Rowling's series, has earned a place in many reader's hearts. His adventures to defeat evil, alongside his friends Hermione and Ron, lasted for seven books. That's a lot to accomplish for a high school student! Rowling's books are the best-selling series of all time. Many readers, young and old, camped out all night at bookstores when each title was released.

The movie series based on the books has also become the most successful of its kind. It has made huge stars of the young cast, and features some of England's most respected older actors. During all of this, Rowling made sure she had creative control

DID YOU KNOW...

J.K. Rowling has introduced many "new" words to the English language through her books, such as Quidditch, muggles, Patronus, and horcrux.

of the movies, and a say in how they turned out. Overall, the popularity of her imaginative Hogwarts world has made her one of the wealthiest and most popular female entertainers in the world. A theme park in Orlando was even built to bring Harry Potter to life further.

STORY HOUR

Rowling holding a copy of her famous creation: Harry Potter and the Sorcerer's Stone.

When the idea for a book about an outcast young boy first came to her, Rowling was riding on a train. She began to craft her first novel right away, but many setbacks lay in her path. Her marriage ended and Rowling was left to take care of her young daughter alone. She said she was "poor

21

BIRTH OF A BOOK

as it is possible to be in modern Britain, without being homeless."

In between working on a school course, Rowling often went to cafés to write, and continued with her book. Her beloved mother passed away, too. In response, she made Harry Potter's orphan experience as realistic as she could. To the waiters clearing her table, Rowling must have seemed like someone down on her luck. No one could have known that the best-selling author in the world was actually the quiet woman scribbling away over a notebook. "Rock bottom became a solid foundation on which I rebuilt my life," Rowling says.

Even after J.K. Rowling found an agent for her finished manuscript, the novel was rejected 12 times before finding a publisher. However, soon after being published in Britain, *Harry Potter and the Philosopher's Stone* attracted attention, awards, and big sales. A publisher in the U.S. bought the rights, and suddenly, everyone in the world was reading *Harry Potter*. The relatable characters, witty writing style, and uniqueness of its fictional world really connected with readers. Without advertising, readers passed the books on to friends and family, and their popularity grew.

Even though Rowling has said many times that the series is truly finished, she is still busy writing. In 2012, she published *The Casual Vacancy*, a novel for adults that became a best-seller. At this point, her name alone has the power to command attention on any book cover.

J.K. Rowling is currently working on two more books, which she hopes to finish soon. For fans that can't let go, she created Pottermore.com, an online Harry Potter world. A smart businesswoman, Rowling made her website the exclusive place to purchase Potter eBooks and digital audio.

The success of Harry Potter as a book and movie phenomenon has led to more wildly successful book series by women. Suzanne Collins' *Hunger Games* trilogy and Stephenie Meyers' *Twilight* series have both sold millions of copies, and also inspired popular movies. Although very different in theme from the Potter books, both series feature young adult characters and creative fantasy worlds. They also have female characters in an even more central role. It is clear that female writers are capable of creating inspiring worlds that readers of both genders can enjoy. Add that to their

Stephenie Meyers' popular Twilight series is about vampires living in a small Western Washington town.

muscle in the marketplace, and Jennifer Weiner's call for more respect definitely seems right. At this very moment, the publishing world is holding its breath, waiting for the next runaway hit—and chances are, the author of that hit will be a woman.

25

CHAPTER 4
FUNNY GIRLS

In 2008, Sarah Palin and Hillary Clinton faced off at the podium, giving speeches as the audience laughed and clapped. Except... the two women were actually Tina Fey and Amy Poehler, two comics impersonating the famous politicians. Both of them took on funny accents and hairstyles in order to earn laughs from the crowd at *Saturday Night Live*. It was one of the most successful episodes the show had ever aired.

For many, comedy is still seen as a "boy's club." In fact, some people, including other comics, insist that women "just aren't funny." In her best-selling book,

Bossypants, Tina Fey wrote about her early years as a comic, and the fact that most directors only wanted one woman per sketch. They thought the show would be dragged down if more than one woman was in the scene.

During her years in the *Second City Comedy Troupe* in Chicago, Fey first learned to write comedy, and met Poehler. "Amy made it clear that she wasn't there to be cute. She wasn't there to play wives and girlfriends in the boys' scenes," she

POLITICAL HUMOR

Tina Fey and Amy Poehler spoofing Sarah Palin and Hillary Clinton on Saturday Night Live.

recalled. This is something Fey could relate to, because she didn't want to play the wives and girlfriends of the male actors, either. She wanted to make people laugh, period.

Both comics were successful at *Second City*, and Amy Poehler also performed with a group called the *Upright Citizens Brigade* in New York City. Later, the two friends met again at *Saturday Night Live,* a historic television show that has aired for many years. Tina Fey worked as one of the only female writers on staff, and became very popular as the co-host of "Weekend Update," a pretend news show. In 2000, she became the first female head writer of the show. As the two performed together and were joined

ON SET

Tina Fey co-hosting "Weekend Update" with Jimmy Fallon.

UPDATEWEEKENDUP

by other comics like Maya Rudolph and Kristen Wiig, more sketches relied on women to get the laughs. In fact, women were stealing the show.

When Tina Fey left the SNL cast in 2006, it was to produce, write, and star in a television show of her very own. Female show creators are rare, but Tina relied on her experience as a writer on SNL to create the idea for her show, *30 Rock*. *30 Rock* goes behind the scenes and creates a humorous portrait of what it could be like for a woman to run a television show. Along with Alec Baldwin as her difficult—and witty—boss, Tina Fey's character is always running around backstage, dealing with the other actors and the entertainment industry. Many of the laughs come from her poking just a little bit of fun at herself. In some episodes, her character admits that it is hard to be a woman in her career. Through hard work, however, her show still makes it on the air every week.

Meanwhile, *30 Rock* paved the way for Amy Poehler to create her own show, *Parks & Recreation*. Another show that has been loved by critics, *Parks & Recreation* is also about a woman in a mostly male field. Poehler's fictional character works in city government, and is surrounded by a team of quirky, yet lovable co-workers. During the show, she becomes the first female town council member. Speaking of female comic styles, Poehler remarked, "I've said this before, that, when you're in school and you're the class clown, men are really good at making fun of other people and women are really good at making fun of themselves." This is something both she and Tina Fey brought to their television shows, and may be why so many people feel they can relate to their characters.

What's next for Fey and Poehler? They have both starred in movies, and will host the Golden Globe

Awards together in 2013. They aren't the only funny women to make their mark, though. In 2011, Kristen Wiig wrote and starred in a movie called *Bridesmaids*. It was a huge hit and proved once again that women can be very funny and attract lots of people to the theatre. The cast featured mostly women of all ages, sizes, and ethnicities – a comedy dream team. Then, young Indian-American comic Mindy Kaling followed in the footsteps of Tina Fey and Amy Poehler.

WITTY WOMEN

Amy Poehler with Aubrey Plaza and Rashida Jones, two of the other female cast members on Parks and Recreation.

She moved from acting in, and writing, episodes of *The Office,* to creating her own show called *The Mindy Project.* She writes, stars in, and produces the show herself, and has also written a successful memoir called *Is Everyone Hanging Out Without Me? (And Other Concerns).*

Instead of claiming that "women aren't funny," television networks now hope to copy the success of *30 Rock* and *Parks & Recreation.* More and more shows now star women in stronger roles than in the past. More and more women are also working behind the scenes to write and produce movies and television. Now *that's* something that can bring a smile to anyone's face.

CHAPTER 5
THE INTERNET AGE

The internet now entertains more people than television, movies, music, and books… mostly because all of those things can be found online! From iPads to computers to phones, people

PHONE CHECK

Handheld electronic devices keep people connected to the internet no matter where they are.

today are able to listen to music, watch videos, and read articles on the go. Technology and the internet have often been seen as a man's world. However, more and more smart women are using the internet to entertain and gain fans.

Arianna Huffington was a long-time figure in political writing and media when she saw the chance to create something new online. In 2005, she founded an online news source, blog, and community called *The Huffington Post*. *The Huffington Post* covers everything from politics to celebrity gossip to health. Since being founded, millions of people have visited the website and become members. Members are able to comment on articles and join the online community. This unique model quickly made Huffington's website one of the most popular on the web. In 2012 it was voted the number-one most popular political website on the internet, and it is also the first website of its kind to win a Pulitzer Prize.

Many people, including members of *The Huffington Post* community, are able to write content for the website. Because of this, writers are able to gain followers from writing for "*Huffpost.*" In 2011, Huffington agreed to a huge deal with AOL. The company purchased her website for $315 million and she became the president and editor-in-chief of The Huffington Post Media Group. Her influence is now even bigger, because she oversees other AOL websites such as *Tech-Crunch* and *Moviefone*.

SUCCESSFUL SMILES

Arianna Huffington attending a film premiere in Los Angeles.

GOOD NEWS...

You can blog anywhere!

Alongside political sites such as *The Huffington Post*, female-based community websites are the fastest-growing on the internet. More women are logging on than ever before, and they are looking to be entertained by things they care about. In 2007, a team of female editors created a site called *Jezebel,* which is a spin-off of a larger website. The women who wrote and edited *Jezebel* "wanted to make the sort of women's magazine we'd want to read." Covering fashion, relationships, and fashion in a fresh, funny way has brought many fans to the site. The young women who write articles for the site do not just write articles about "how to lose weight" or "how to get the guy." Instead, they focus on funny, inspiring, and even controversial stories and opinions.

Women continue to join online communities and contribute their own writing. In response, Lisa Stone, Elisa Camahort Page, and Jory Des Jardins founded the *BlogHer* network. They founded the network because they wanted an answer to the question: "Where are all the women bloggers?" Each year, female bloggers and blog readers from all over the world gather for *BlogHer* conventions. There, they can share friendships with other bloggers and gain more followers and advertisers for their blogs. With 50 million visitors per month, *BlogHer*

DID YOU KNOW...

A "blog" is a website that can be updated with new writing and content frequently. A "blogger" is someone who writes a blog.

helps women to find their own voices and community. For example, a gardener in Oakland, California, might find a great gardening blog written by a woman from Rhode Island. Even without meeting, *BlogHer* can connect the two women and give them a chance to share gardening tips.

Cyberspace can also be a unique way for musicians to sell records, and for performers to get attention. Just look at musician Amanda Palmer. Although she had released CDs with a record label before, she became frustrated with the process. Using Twitter as her platform, Palmer has invited fans to secret shows and publicized her merchandise. In one night alone, she was able to make $11,000 selling T-shirts using Twitter. In contrast, she says, the amount she made on her big record label album was much less. In July of 2012, she released new music and merchandise on the website Bandcamp. This

Catherine Harris-White and Stasia Irons of Thee Satisfaction.

site allows musicians to post their music for fans to listen to and buy. In just three minutes, Palmer's fans had rushed online to buy $15,000 worth of digital music. Other musicians—such as the girl rap group Thee Satisfaction, from Seattle—use YouTube, Bandcamp, and MySpace to get their music out there. This helps boost record sales and the amount of fans attending their concerts.

There are many websites that can help performers and artists gain fans.

These days, writers, actors, and singers often create Facebook pages and blogs to connect to their fans. Famous entertainers like Oprah have their own websites, and word spreads quickly from fan to fan. As more women log on and use their phones to connect to the internet, it will be interesting to see how entertainment changes. It has never been easy to become a star, but the internet provides a new "stage." Women entertainers are entering a new era, where they can become even more powerful than before.